THE LITTLE BOOK OF
internet dating

GW00632153

Written by Tim Collins
Edited by Philippa Wingate
Illustrated by Paul Middlewick
Designed by Angie Allison
Cover designed by
www.blacksheep-uk.com

With thanks to www.speeddater.co.uk

THE LITTLE BOOK OF
internet dating

Michael O'Mara Books Limited

First published in Great Britain in 2005 by
Michael O'Mara Books Limited, 9 Lion Yard,
Tremadoc Road, London SW4 7NQ
www.mombooks.com

A CIP catalogue record for this book is available
from the British Library

ISBN 1-84317-173-2

1 3 5 7 9 10 8 6 4 2

Printed and bound in Great Britain
by William Clowes Ltd, Beccles, Suffolk

Contents

Introduction

Just do it

I know, I know. You're not the kind of person who has to use dating websites. You're not a computer nerd, and you're not considering using 'HanSoloFan' as your screen name.

It's just that a mate suggested you try Internet dating and you're sort of maybe considering it.

Well, guess what?
There are thousands of people out
there just like you. They don't live
with their parents. They don't
speak Klingon. And they won't
spend the first date talking about
wireless networking.

So how do you meet them?
Well, you sign up to a dating site,
you exchange emails and, if you
like them, you arrange a face-to-

face date. Quite simple, really. But, like anything else, there are a few things you should know before you start. Without following the correct 'netiquette', you could be in danger of coming on too strong and seeming like a bunny boiler, or being so nonchalant that you don't get noticed at all.

And that's where this book comes in. It'll tell you everything you need to know about online dating.

Whether you choose to follow or ignore the suggestions in this book is up to you, but I would at least urge you to give online dating a try. After all, you never know. There might even be someone as sexy, intelligent, and likeable as you out there.

Oh, go on...

Ten good reasons to
give web dating a try

- You can meet someone new
  without putting your face on or
  wearing your pulling pants.

- You can meet someone new
  without having to queue, pay
  four quid for a drink, or shout
  above pumping Euro techno.

- You don't have to convince your friend to come along with you, and then shamelessly dump them when you meet someone.

- You can decide if you fancy someone while sober.

- You don't have to suffer the horrors of going out on the pull, such as chat-up lines.

- You can avoid the shame of your friends matching you up with a dweeb, which not only wastes an evening but gives you an uncomfortable insight into what your friends think of you.

- If you work in an office, you can date from your desk all day, and it will look like you're working hard.

- The potential fallout is far less

severe than dating someone from your workplace or immediate circle of friends.

- It relies less on luck than waiting to bump into someone on the street and fall in love with them, like in a Meg Ryan film.

- You can make email contact with lots of new people at once, and increase your chances of finding someone right.

FAQs

What do I need to get started?

Well, a computer with web connection would help. It's worth registering a new email address at somewhere like Yahoo! or Hotmail, even if you're using a dating site that provides an internal mailbox. A digital camera or scanner is useful for submitting your picture, although most photo-processing shops can put your photos on to a CD.

How do I choose on online dating site?

There are hundreds of online dating sites out there, so it's important to visit a few before plumping for a particular one.

Although free Internet-dating sites exist, those with a subscription tend to be better, and you're less likely to meet a pikey who suggests a date in Kansas Fried Chicken.

The first choice you'll have to make is between a general dating site and one tailored to a specific group. Do you only want to meet people of the same ethnic background as you? Or the same religion? Or the same height?

If you do, there'll be a site out there for you. But you'll get a better choice if you keep your options open, especially if you live in a relatively unpopulated area.

You'll also find that the features of dating sites vary considerably. Some have chat rooms where you can meet lots of members at once, some let you initiate instant messenger conversations, and others show you the last time a member logged in or updated their profile.

Choosing a dating site can be quite a laborious process, but you should take the time to find one you like before handing over any money. Ultimately, there's no substitute for Googling your way around the web, reading profiles, taking tours and signing up for free trials.

Who is online?

If you think of online daters as thirty-something blokes who still live with their parents, and as women who talk to their cats, think again. Online dating has expanded rapidly over the last couple of years, with some estimates suggesting that over half of the single adult population of the UK have tried it. Given this mainstream acceptance, it's no surprise that the quality of people involved is high.

After all, you're considering it, aren't you?
On the whole, online daters (at least on the pay sites) tend to be reasonably well off but 'time poor' professionals who don't get to meet enough single people socially, and who don't want to 'dip their pen in the office ink'.

But you only need to look at the various profiles on the web to see the wide range of people who are out there.

What do I need to submit?

What you will need to submit varies from site to site. Some ask you to complete a personality test, some ask you to write a pithy headline describing yourself, and some even let you submit audio messages and video clips.

However, all online dating sites will ask you to submit a

 username and
a profile.

As for your username, it's better to protect your anonymity and invent one, rather than use your real name. You can choose anything from 'Zoe2006' to 'Hotslut69' or 'Gagging4it', depending on the kind of responses and dates you're looking for.

Your photo and profile are
discussed over the next couple of
chapters.

Your photo

Submitting a photo

Although it's possible to submit a profile without a photo, you'll get a lot more responses if you include one. Indeed, some sites now feature a search option which filters out those who haven't posted photos.

The truth is that in real life we draw a lot of information about people from their appearance, and online dating is no different.

So digging out a snap that's flattering but not too misleading is essential.

A few common types of online dating photo

Passport photo

Pros: Makes you look unpretentious.

Cons: Not even Brad Pitt would look attractive in one.

Holiday photo

Pros: Makes you look well travelled.

Cons: Sunburn, shades and sweat patches are never good. And it's always best to avoid snaps of yourself 'propping up' the Leaning Tower of Pisa.

Black-and-white photo

Pros: Makes you look arty.

Cons: Makes you look pretentious. Either that or people will assume that this is a really old photo of you.

Picture that you've jazzed up using Photoshop (no, really - people actually do this)

Pros: Might meet fellow Photoshop enthusiasts.

Cons: Trying way too hard. Especially if you've added a background of swirling psychedelic colours and a logo of your name.

*Photo of
yourself posing
with an expensive
possession, like a
sports car*

Pros: Shows you're rich.

Cons: You'll attract gold-diggers.

Photo of yourself posing with your computer, or looking into your webcam

Pros: Shows you're web-literate.

Cons: We sort of knew that.

Photo of yourself frowning

Pros: Makes you seem pensive and contemplative.

Cons: Smile, you miserable bastard. Everybody else seems to manage it.

Photo of a model you've scanned in from a magazine

Pros: You'll get a lot of responses.

Cons: All these people will realize that you're a weird, deluded liar when they meet you, and suddenly remember that they're late for another appointment.

40

Hints on submitting your photo

You'll get a better response if you choose a straightforward and natural shot rather than a cheesy, posed one.

Avoid any photos where you're so small that no one can see your face. Even if you're in front of a really nice landmark.

Avoid submitting half a photo of you and your ex on holiday. Or half a wedding photo.

Submit a recent photo. As with all stages of the Internet-dating process, dishonesty is ultimately pretty pointless. After all, the revelation that you're ten years older than you'd claimed isn't the best start to a date.

If you can, submit a photo taken outside. Natural light is often more flattering than the harsh light of a flash.

If you're posting more than one photo, try to include a variety of close-ups and wider shots. Posting a sequence of catalogue-style poses that you've taken one after the other is not a good idea.

If you're taking a shot especially for your profile, get a friend to take it for you, or at least find a camera with a timer. Nothing says 'dangerous, creepy loner' more than a photo of you holding out your camera at arm's length.

And finally, avoid any photos of yourself sitting on your bed and strumming an acoustic guitar. *Please.*

Your profile

Questionnaires and essays

For some people, sitting down and writing about themselves will be the most daunting part of the whole Internet-dating process. The only thing they'll have had to write about themselves in the past will have been their CV. And this time, listing all your previous experience is *not* a good idea.

Most dating sites ask you to answer a series of multiple-choice questions before prompting you to write an essay or series of essays about yourself and the kind of person you're looking for.

It's always tempting to dash off a couple of bland sentences for the essay section, especially if you've just answered a long questionnaire. But this may be a mistake.

Consider your own approach to reading profiles for a minute. The chances are that after checking out the photos, you probably scan through the questionnaires to the essay sections, to find out what people have to say about themselves. However many questions you've answered about your star sign, pets and body piercings, a surprising or amusing turn of phrase in an essay section is the thing that will get you noticed.

So take time over the essay part. Redraft it until you're happy with it and send it to a friend to read (although be careful not to send it out as an all-staff email by mistake).

It's also worth altering your profile every now and then, especially if you're using a site that displays search results in order of the most recently updated.

Profile dos and don'ts

Do: Give a truthful description
of yourself.

Don't: Lie. This is a profile, not a
CV. Any dishonesty will
soon become apparent
when you meet someone
face-to-face. And this goes
for tastes and hobbies as
well as physical descriptions
- there's no point in

pretending
you're into
opera if you
prefer the Men
& Motors channel,
or Footballers' Wives.

Do: Give a brief overview of
your good points or
achievements.

Don't: Talk yourself up relentlessly. Again, this isn't a CV. The kind of language that might make you seem like a dynamic go-getter in a job interview will make you look like a show-off here. A little self-effacing humour will go a lot further than a list of all the firms who've headhunted you recently.

Do: Give a general description of the kind of person you're looking for.

Don't: Make your description an intimidating list of positive qualities. You'll only attract arrogant people.

Do: Browse through the essays already posted on the site. Make a note of any phrases or sentences that catch your attention.

Don't: Copy and paste someone else's essay because you can't be bothered writing one yourself.

Do: Be honest.

Don't: Be too honest. There are some things that are probably best left out for now, such as:

'**I've recently been dumped and am seeking someone to listen to endless rants about "that bitch/bastard".**'

'**I'll cry if you don't take my calls at work.**'

'I finished a five-year relationship a couple of weeks ago and I'm looking for a revenge shag.'

'I've recently had a restraining order put out against me.'

'I'm an attractive and intelligent man who loves

dancing and clothes shopping. The sooner I admit I'm gay and stop wasting everyone's time, the better.'

Avoiding clichés

Your profile will be read along with hundreds of others, so the worst thing you can do is be the same as everyone else.

Try to avoid sentences like:

'I can't believe I'm doing this!'

'I'm not the sort of person who usually uses dating agencies.'

'I'm looking for someone to be my partner and my best friend.'

'I enjoy romantic candlelit dinners/walking along the beach at sunset.'

'I work hard and play hard.'

'There simply isn't enough space here for me to fit in everything about my life!!!'

Even more annoying than all of these, however, is the generic list. Lots of people fill their essays with a list of adjectives like 'fun', 'honest' and 'intelligent', and a list of interests like 'music', 'travel' and 'reading'. I'm sure all this is true. But if this is all you're going to write, you may as well copy and paste your essay from the thousands of identical ones out there.

If you want to grab someone's attention, be specific. If someone finds out that you're into music it probably won't make them respond, but if they discover that you were at the same gig they were last March, they may.

So, illustrate what you write with examples:

'I'm into music…'
What kind?
What was the last
live concert you went to?

'I travel a lot…'
Where have you been to recently?
Where would you most like to
visit?

'I'm into sport…'
Which sports? Watching them or
participating in them?

'I'm into film…'
What kinds of film? What are
your favourite films?

'I like reading…'
What type of books? Who's your
favourite author?

'I'm fun...'
What fun things do you do?

'I have a good sense of humour...'
Go on then. Write something funny.

'I'm intelligent...'
You won't need to tell people this

if you've written your essay in an intelligent way.

'I'm honest...'
I hope so. Otherwise the rest of your profile is untrue and you're wasting everyone's time. Again, you shouldn't really need to include this.

Common euphemisms

In addition to the clichés I've
mentioned above, there are a
number of profile euphemisms
that have become in-jokes among
Internet daters...

Communicative – loud

Distinguished – old

Drinks once in a while – alcoholic

Free spirit – commitment-phobe

Huggable/cuddly – fat

Loose cannon – tosser

Mature – old

Open-minded – kinky

Outgoing – loud

Rubenesque – fat

Seeks soulmate – stalker/bunny boiler

Thirtyish – thirty-nine

Very attractive – arrogant

Voluptuous – see 'Rubenesque'

Young at heart – old

A few style tips

- DO NOT WRITE YOUR ESSAY WITH THE CAPS LOCK ON. THIS WILL MAKE YOU SEEM ANGRY.

- Try to avoid too many exclamation marks!!! F. Scott Fitzgerald said that using exclamation marks is like laughing at your own jokes!!!

69

- It is better where possible to use short sentences rather than long rambling ones as they tend to be a bit easier for the reader to take in.

- Run you're essay though a spell check and proofread it. You'll will be surprised how many people fail to do this.

- BTW don't overdo the web acronyms. FYI not everyone knows what these stand for.

Making contact

The rules of netiquette

There's a famous scene in the 1996 movie *Swingers* where the characters discuss the unwritten laws of dating, such as the 'industry standard' time to leave between obtaining a girl's phone number and calling her.

Online dating has its own unwritten rules too; follow these steps if you want to avoid looking like a newbie:

1. If you like someone's profile, send them a quick introductory email. And by the way, ladies, this isn't a school disco – you're allowed to make the first move too.

2. Don't include your mobile number or suggest meeting up for a date at this stage.

3. Wait patiently for a reply. Don't bombard them with follow-up emails before they've had a chance to respond.

4. If you haven't had a reply from them after a few days, try a follow-up email.

5. If you still don't get a reply from them, cross them off your list and move on.

6. Exchanging emails with more than one person at a time is not just OK, it's assumed. So 'parallel date', and increase your chances of success.

7. Only after you've been exchanging emails for a few days or weeks is it the right

time to suggest taking things offline (see page 100).

8. Arrange an initial phone call, or series of calls, first.

9. If the calls go well, move on to a face-to-face date.

10. If you find true, everlasting love, remember to remove your profile.

Dos and don'ts for exchanging emails

There are a few dos and don'ts that you should observe when contacting potential dates…

Do: Send a brief initial email suggesting they check out your profile.

Don't: Send a long, rambling email regurgitating your profile.

Do: Send another email if you haven't received a reply after a few days.

Don't: Send an angry email if you haven't received a reply within a couple of minutes.

Do: Proofread your email before sending it.

Don't: Point out the spelling and grammar mistakes in someone else's email. If you're absolutely sure you could never date someone who splits infinitives, it's probably best not to reply at all.

Do: Mention that they look good in their photograph.

Don't: Make crude sexual comments. Remarks that might seem flirtatious in conversation can come across as aggressive when written down. Even if you follow them with an emoticon like :-)

Do: Sign off your email with something casual like 'Hope to hear from you soon', or just your first name.

Don't: Sign off your email with 'Love', 'Yours forever' or 'Shag you later'.

What to write

It's easy to make your initial
email to someone stand out – just
respond to something specific in
their profile. This might sound
obvious, but it's amazing how
many people don't do it.

As you'll see from the first few
messages you get, lots of people
send out an identical introductory
email to all contacts which is

largely about themselves. Aside from making them seem a little self-obsessed, this can also give the impression that they haven't even read the profile they're responding to.

So, include lots of complimentary references to their profile, and get a dialogue going with some relevant open-ended questions.

What not to write

Obviously there are no real rules
for the kind of things you should
be discussing at this stage. If
you're obsessed with collecting
toby jugs and recreating historical
battles, I'm sure there's someone
out there for you. But there are
some things that are probably best
avoided for now:

'I hope to God this works out – I couldn't bear to get hurt again.'

'I like walking in the countryside too. We'll be able to do plenty of that when we're married.'

'This is an exciting opportunity for both of us. Call my PA and she'll set up a meeting.'

'I broke up with my last boyfriend in 1998, but I'm pretty much over it now.'

'What do you think we should call our first child if it's a girl?'

'I've written a poem about you...'

'Are you the Jane who likes rock climbing or the Jane who likes crime fiction? I can't remember.'

'I feel like we've always known each other.'

'Please. I'm desperate.'

Warning signs

The line between being sensibly cautious and paranoid is a fine one. But there are some strange people out there, so keep an eye out for these warning signs:

Warning sign: Your date claims not to have a home phone number.

Possible reasons: Could be a married person looking for an affair; could just be really poor.

Warning sign: Your date refuses to give out any information about their personal life.

Possible reasons: Could be a married person looking for an affair; could have no life.

Warning sign: Your date never seems to be available in the evenings.

Possible reasons: Could be a married person looking for an affair; could have a busy social life; could be a night watchman.

Warning sign: Your date bombards you

with emails and pushes for a face-to-face date straight away.

Possible reasons: Could be a rebounding newbie unfamiliar with netiquette; could be desperate.

Warning sign: Your date's online photo contains lava lamps, Betamax tapes and copies of *Today* newspaper.

Possible reasons: Could have cool retro tastes; could be older than they're claiming.

Warning sign: Your date has given inconsistent information in their profile and emails.

Possible reasons: Could be a compulsive liar; could be an online prankster stringing you along; could have made a genuine mistake. Ask them to explain themselves.

Warning sign: Your date claims to be a Nigerian millionaire who needs your bank details so he can temporarily move some money into your account.

Possible reasons: Might be a bit dishonest. Just a hunch.

E-dumping

Internet dating is an unusually accelerated process, and you may find yourself having to brush off more people in your first few months than you had to in all your years of face-to-face dating.

If you've been emailing someone but you don't think it's going to work, don't waste their time by stringing them along. Just be grown up about it and send them a note explaining that you don't want them to contact you any more.

Failing that, be a coward and use one of these handy excuses:

'I'm getting really serious with someone else I've met online, and we've agreed to cut off all our other contacts.'

'I've started to question my sexuality recently, and I don't think it's fair for you to be around me at this difficult stage.'

'I might as well be honest – I'm ten years older/stone heavier/inches shorter than I've been claiming.'

'I've recently joined a religious cult that only lets me date other members.'

'I've had a look at your profile and photo again and I've realized that you're totally out of my league.'

If they don't take the hint, and send you an email which says something like, 'If we can't be together in this world, it will have to be the next one,' get your site to block any further emails from them.

As you've probably guessed, the flipside to all this is that you'll have to get used to being e-dumped too.

Clearly, rejection is never a nice thing. But getting blown out online isn't the same as getting blown out in real life. You haven't invested too much time and effort in them, and it's easy enough to press delete and move on to the next person.

Going offline

Moving from online romance to offline romance

As was mentioned at the start of this book, the good thing about Internet dating is that you only need to bother going on an actual date if your email contact has gone well. In theory, you should be able to avoid the kind of date where you both spend the evening reading the menu over and over again while desperately trying to think of something to say.

Of course, dating disasters do still happen. But there are a few things you can do to ensure that they don't happen to you:

- Only agree to a date if you genuinely want to meet someone. Don't agree to go just because you're scared of rejecting them.

- Call your date a couple of times before meeting them face to face. This should give you a much better idea of whether you'll click.

- Set up a lunchtime coffee date before going on a full evening date. If it goes badly, you've only wasted half an hour and the price of a tall skinny mocha with cream.

- Always give yourself an escape route. Say you've got to be somewhere else in an hour's time. This 'appointment' can always be mysteriously cancelled if things are going well.

- Avoid meeting in a trendy bar where the music's so loud you can't hear each other.

- Oh, and try to avoid talking with your mouth full, answering your mobile mid-conversation and laughing so hard you snort wine out of your nose.

Safety tips

Like any major social trend, Internet dating has generated its fair share of scare stories and urban myths. Will you have all your money stolen by a confidence trickster? Will your date brainwash you into joining a cult?

Probably not. But all types of dating entail real dangers that

- Trust your instincts. If you have a bad feeling about someone, don't risk taking it any further.

One final rule of netiquette

So you've emailed someone, phoned them, met for coffee, gone on an evening date and now you've agreed to get serious and remove your profiles.

The final rule of netiquette is that if you've agreed to remove your profile, you actually do it.

After all, your new partner (how good does that sound?) will know exactly how to check.

The jargon
of Internet dating

Even the net-savvy are likely to come across a few unfamiliar terms when they start dating online. This section should help you decode some of them.

You might even be tempted to slip a couple into your own emails or instant-messenger chats. But be warned that too much web-speak will make you look like a nerd.

Write in straightforward, conversational English and you'll come across as much more approachable.

ASL? or A/S/L – A request for your 'Age, Sex and Location' used in chat rooms. It can also be a request for 'Age, Size and Location' in gay chat rooms, which is quite a neat use of an otherwise redundant 'S'.

AWYR – Web speak for 'Awaiting Your Reply'.

Block user – A useful feature of some dating sites that lets you prevent stalkers and bunny boilers from contacting you ever again.

BRB – Web acronym for 'Be Right Back'.

E-dumping – Ending an online relationship. Theoretically entails less disappointment or guilt than real-life dumping.

F2F – Email speak for 'Face-to-Face'.

Googlestalking – Using Google to search for information about a date before meeting them. Could result in your date being impressed with your enthusiasm. Could just result in them being freaked out.

GSOH – Personal-ad. acronym for 'Good Sense Of Humour'. Often used by people with no discernible SOH at all.

GU – Dating speak for 'Geographically Undesirable'. Most Internet dating sites let you tailor your search to people within a certain distance from your house, so you don't waste time emailing someone you couldn't realistically date in person.

HAK – Email acronym for 'Hugs And Kisses'.

Hide profile – A feature of some online dating sites that lets you go online without others knowing. Especially useful if you don't want anyone to know that you spend your Friday and Saturday nights on the web.

IRL – Email acronym for 'In Real Life'. You know, that place where you have to say things out loud instead of typing.

ISO – Personal-ad acronym for 'In Search Of...'

LOL – Web acronym for 'Laughing Out Loud'. Not a good thing to follow your own jokes with. Confusingly, it can also be used to mean 'Lots Of Love' or 'Lots Of Luck'.

LTNS – Email acronym for 'Long Time No See'.

Netiquette – The unwritten rules of online behaviour (see Chapter 4).

Parallel dating – Exchanging emails with more than one date at a time. Perfectly acceptable under the laws of netiquette. Assume that whoever you're emailing is also contacting other people unless you've discussed it and agreed not to.

Photo fraud – The online crime of trying to pass off a photo of someone else as yourself. If you suspect someone of this, ask them to send more photos.

Player – Web slang for a timewaster who is deliberately stringing you along as a practical joke. If you encounter one of these 'cyber-Beadles', report them to your site.

Profile – The information about yourself that you'll be required to submit, usually in response to a questionnaire and an essay question or series of essay questions. Getting this right is an important step to Internet-dating success (see Chapter 3).

Silver surfer – A web-savvy older person (online dating for older people being one of the

most rapidly expanding
areas of the business).

Spamming – Sending out the
same standard email about
yourself to lots of people. Might
seem like a good way to increase
your chances of meeting
someone, but most people will
realize what you're up to and
delete your message. Especially
if it starts 'Dear recipient'.

SWF/SBF – 'Single White Female'/ 'Single Black Female'. These acronyms derive from the time when you had to pay by the word when placing personal ads, and seem a bit redundant now.

Teases – A feature of some online dating sites which lets non-members send you a free standard message. Also known as winks, smiles, icebreakers, whispers and collect calls.

TMI – Web acronym for 'Too Much Information'. Used when people break the laws of netiquette by discussing things like past relationships during the initial stages of email contact.